I Can Accept Others

Doing the Right Thing

Written by Jenette Donovan Guntly

Photographed by Michael Jarrett

GARETH**STEVENS**
GS
PUBLISHING
A World Almanac Education Group Company

Please visit our web site at: www.garethstevens.com
For a free color catalog describing Gareth Stevens Publishing's list of high-quality books
and multimedia programs, call 1-800-542-2595 (USA) or 1-800-387-3178 (Canada).
Gareth Stevens Publishing's fax: (414) 332-3567.

Library of Congress Cataloging-in-Publication Data

Guntly, Jenette Donovan.
   (Everyone is special and unique)
   I can accept others / written by Jenette Donovan Guntly; photographed by Michael Jarrett.
     p. cm. — (Doing the right thing)
   ISBN 0-8368-4244-8 (lib. bdg.)
   1. Respect for persons—Juvenile literature. I. Jarrett, Michael, 1956- . II. Title.
  BJ1533.R42G86   2004
  177'.5—dc22
                                          2004045300

This North American edition first published in 2005 by
Gareth Stevens Publishing
A World Almanac Education Group Company
330 West Olive Street, Suite 100
Milwaukee, WI 53212 USA

This edition copyright © 2005 by Gareth Stevens, Inc. Original edition copyright © 2002 by Creative Teaching Press, Inc.,
P.O. Box 2723, Huntington Beach, CA 92647-0723. First published in the United States in 2002 as *Everyone Is Special and
Unique: Learning about Acceptance* by Creative Teaching Press, Inc. Original text copyright © 2002 by Regina G. Burch.

Photographer: Michael Jarrett
Gareth Stevens designer: Kami M. Koenig

Printed in the United States of America

1 2 3 4 5 6 7 8 9 08 07 06 05 04

I can accept others!

When we all want different things,

we talk our problems through.

We each like different kinds of foods.

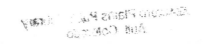

6

We like the same foods, too.

Ginny always wins at games.

I'm happy for my friend.

9

Li has no more tickets left.

We give him some to spend.

Our friends may not be just like us,

but we all get along.

Northern Plains Public Library
Ault Colorado

13

We're different in so many ways,

but we each still belong.

We can all have much more fun
when we are friends with everyone!